Mud of the SOMME

*The first book
of the Fallen Heroes series*

Tim Barrett

Mud of the Somme
The first book of the Fallen Heroes series

Copyright © 2013 by Tim Barrett.
All rights reserved.

No part of this book may be reproduced, transmitted, or distributed in any form or by any means, electronic, mechanical, photocopying, recording, scanning, or otherwise, without the prior written permission of the author.

ISBN-13: 978-0-9923537-0-4

Cover image © Gudellaphoto—Fotolia.com
Cover and interior design: Adina Cucicov,
Flamingo Designs

This book is a work of fiction. All characters in this novel are fictitious. Any resemblance to actual events or locales or persons, living or dead, is entirely coincidental.

*To the ANZAC's who fought
on the Western Front.*

Table of Contents

Introduction. 1919 1
Chapter 1. August 1914 3
Chapter 2. October 1915 7
Chapter 3. October/November 1915 11
Chapter 4. December 1915 15
Chapter 5. January 1916 19
Chapter 6. February 1916 23
Chapter 7. March/April 1916 27
Chapter 8. May 1916 31
Chapter 9. June/July 1916 35
Chapter 10. August 1916 39
Chapter 11. September 1916 43
Chapter 12. October 1916 47
Chapter 13. November 1916 51
Chapter 14. December 1916 55
Epilogue 59
Acknowledgments 61

INTRODUCTION

1919

MY NAME IS Charlie J Hunter. I'm a drover from the Outback. I served in the horrible war in the nasty trenches far from my home.

CHAPTER 1

August 1914

Mud of the SOMME

August 1914

I WAS A young drover when the war began. Dad picked up the paper with the headline WAR DECLARED. I went to town to enlist. I was only fifteen but I said I was nineteen. I thought the Germans were savages and I wanted to fight them.

I rushed into town on Darby hitched to the buggy. I was so fast I nearly crashed into Town Hall. I ran up the steps, into the hall and walked to the Recruiting Officer at the desk.

He said "Son, 'ya really gonna lie to get in? Like to see you try!".

The older boys said "You little wimp, my Dad told me to "kill a hun" hope yours didn't .. ha ha ha"

When I got home Mum was furious.

"You're not going, I don't want you in pieces", she said.

Mum had lost Uncle Samuel in the Boer War with the Queensland Mounted Infantry at Traans Vaal.

Dad said "My dad survived the Boer War, let 'im go".

But then Dad changed his mind and said "Nope, you're too young. The AIF's age limit is 19 to 29".

I commented "those wretched 19 year olds called me a wimp".

I hoped I'd survive this war.

CHAPTER 2

October 1915

 Mud of the SOMME

October 1915

IT WAS HORRIBLE at home. People yelled "coward" or "boo" at me. I was sixteen now and I needed to go to war. The older boys were already at Gallipoli. I tried and tried to go off but Mum found out every time. It was all too much. So one day I decided to join up for good.

The town hall was teeming with volunteers. It was now or never.

"How old are you?" the Officer asked.

"Nineteen, I know I look sixteen", I said.

"Congratulations", he said, "welcome to the 7th Batallion AIF".

At home I broke the news to Mum and Dad. I felt in my pocket. I found a train ticket to Duntroon.

CHAPTER 3

October/November 1915

 Mud of the SOMME

October/November 1915

AT THE STATION, I was boarding the troop train to Duntroon.

Chug, chug, chug .. the train started moving. I waved to Mum and Dad out the window. I was on a train for hours. I arrived at Canberra station where I met Tommy Parker from Bourke.

Me, Tommy and a hundred others were marched through the streets as "recruits" to Duntroon. We went through rigorous training and days went by. We were taught to march, salute, work a gun, tie bayonettes to guns and shoot. We completed training and were given uniforms. Then the next day, we caught a train to Broome then set off on "Mary's Fighter".

CHAPTER 4

December 1915

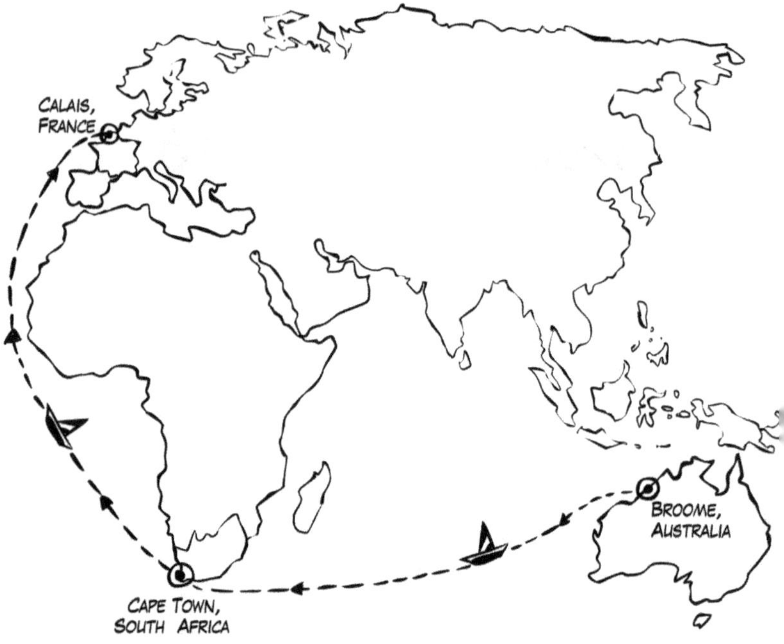
CALAIS,
FRANCE
BROOME,
AUSTRALIA
CAPE TOWN,
SOUTH AFRICA

December 1915

WE ROCKED FROM side to side on the boat. I hated the cramped, dark space in the sleeping quarters. We stopped in South Africa to get our supplies then we rocked and slid our way to France.

We arrived in France on Boxing Day. I saw British soldiers being rushed around from place to place in trucks and trains. Wounded soldiers screamed in pain. Troops had no arms, no legs, no right eye, smashed faces, loss of memory, "shell shock" and dyslexia from schrapnel. Most were gassed and blindfolded, walking around in circles.

CHAPTER 5

January 1916

 Mud of the SOMME

January 1916

WE WERE IN the trenches now, the most horrible and nasty place ever. The shells were so loud they made you fall over in the thick, deep mud.

One day I received a Care package from the Australian Comforts fund. We got pyjamas, socks, beanies, scarves and a magazine.

We got letters from home. Tom said his brother was coming to France from Gallipoli. This was the letter he got.

"Dear Tom, it's horrible here on Skyros Island, there are so many wounded. Our regiment is nearly leaving, about 6.30 tonight. We've lost half our regiment at that hellhole Gallipoli. Many died during our evacuation. We got a chance to bury them. I've got to pack. Stay safe. Your brother, Peter".

CHAPTER 6

February 1916

 Mud of the SOMME

February 1916

IN THOSE HORRIBLE trenches, we saw huge rats. They were as big as cats, even bigger! Think of a normal rat in a house, well that's small. We had no rat traps or poison so we blew them up with cordite, an explosive substance.

We dreaded going "over the top". Our nightmares became real one day. The Sergeant blew the whistle when the first ray of sunlight came over a shell hole. We ran out of the trench. Bullets whizzed over our helmets, machine guns rattled on in this hell on earth. We scurried back into the trench like rabbits during a forest shooting. Many men died while being carried to safety on stretchers.

CHAPTER 7

March/April 1916

Mud of the SOMME

March/April 1916

ONE DAY WE were standing to attention on Parade outside our dugouts and were told some news.

"Atenshun", snapped our RSM. "We've received news from HQ that we will make an advance across the Somme River. Our Top Brass wishes you good luck. Dismissed".

Was I to go into battle?

During the next couple of weeks, talk of a battle seemed exciting. It was the main agenda. Would there be medals? Would we all capture hordes of Germans?

CHAPTER 8

May 1916

Mud of the SOMME

May 1916

AFTER A WHILE, the excited feeling of a battle died. We would get slaughtered like a lamb to go to a butcher and become your dinner. We thought HQ were crazy for not calling people for reinforcement.

Two days later, reinforcements arrived. They were, in my opinion, too young to serve.

"Watch out Fritz", I thought, "cause you are about to meet the Aussies".

CHAPTER 9

June/July 1916

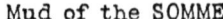

Mud of the SOMME

June/July 1916

IT WAS ONLY a month til the Somme Offensive that would change history forever. We thought the Fritz would run away. The truth is, they'd launch their secret weapon if defeat was possible.

Our aim was to capture the village of Pozieries. At midnight, we stormed the village. Machine guns opened up from the Village Square and church.

Amongst the onslaught, Tommy was gunned down. His last words were "give my love to Pete and Mum".

CHAPTER 10

August 1916

# Mud of the SOMME

August 1916

FOR FORTY FIVE days in Pozieres we were in a horrible fight for our land. I was hiding in an old fruit stall at the village square.

"There has to be a twist", I thought.

I crept into the Town Hall with stealthness. It was dark and eerie, with no-one in sight. Then came a high pitched whistle. A shell! I ran out of the Town Hall and seconds later the shell exploded. My luck was with me that day, but would not come later in the battle.

CHAPTER 11

September 1916

Mud of the SOMME

September 1916

ON SEPTEMBER 2ᴺᴰ we were relieved. Many good men had died, including most of the new members of our Batallion. The rest of us were saved. The battle was over.

We were walking back from the town when there was another high pitched whistle, The next thing I remember was I was thrown into the air and then passed out.

CHAPTER 12

October 1916

 Mud of the SOMME

October 1916

A FEW WEEKS later I woke up in a hospital only a few kilometres from where I passed out.

"Where am I?", I asked the nurse.

She explained how I had sustained bruises on my legs and I had experienced a severe concussion.

Men next to me were crying for their parents or screaming out loud. The smell of filthy bandages was hanging in the air.

A seventeen year old couldn't bear to see what I saw.

CHAPTER 13

November 1916

Mud of the SOMME

November 1916

I WAS FORMALLY discharged from hospital after a few weeks. No-one liked being in that smelly, crowded place. The nurse told me to be careful with the concussion and the banging in my head.

In the trenches, I found out that twelve men went to hospital with pneumonia, and more with diarrhea. Things had changed very much since I had been injured.

CHAPTER 14

December 1916

Mud of the SOMME

ONE MORNING I woke up and the trenches were eerie and silent. I thought the war had ended, but somebody told me it was Christmas Day.

The sky was gray and the temperatures made me shiver like I was in the Artic. Then I heard a call from the other side of no man's land–"Merry Christmas".

It was the Germans who called over the smell of rotten corpses. Then they started singing Silent Night. We joined into the German's peaceful harmony. One German threw over a box of Cigarettes with a message "A gift from the other side".

We all had tears of joy on this frosty Christmas morning. For one day our enemies became our friends. I looked up in wonder and saw the birds chirping as they flew over the mud and horror.

December 1916

CHARLES JEFFREY HUNTER
7TH BATTALLION AIF

YOU HAVE BEEN FORMALLY DISCHARGED FROM THE AUSTRALIAN IMPERIAL FORCE. YOU SERVED YOUR KING AND COUNTRY AND THEREFORE DISCHARGED ON THIS DAY SIXTH OF JANUARY, NINETEEN HUNDRED AND SEVENTEEN DUE TO MENTAL INJURIES.

British War Office London

Monash
GENERAL MONASH
6TH JANUARY 1917

Epilogue

I WAS SO relieved when I got discharged away from Hell. It was really hard to settle into life back at the station. I had nightmares and every night I woke sweating. During the day, whilst out in town, I saw returned soldiers with horrifying injuries and I couldn't bear what I saw.

I eventually got psychology treatment in Melbourne. I'm now in the recovery state of treatment. At least I'm recovering, not back where I was before. The future (I hope) will be better for me, and my family.

Acknowledgments

TIM BEING TIM didn't see any requirement to acknowledge or thank anyone other than the men to which he dedicated this book, but we couldn't let the opportunity pass to express our thanks and appreciation to some very special people.

We remember only too well the little boy who couldn't hold a pencil and for years found writing to be torture. Today, writing is one of Tim's greatest joys and this would not have been possible without them.

To Louise, Kirsten and Tim's teachers at Mudgeeraba State School, we are forever grateful for your patience, kindness and dedication. He would not be the remarkable boy he is today without having had you all in his life.

With our thanks & gratitude always,
Kris & Graham.

www.ingramcontent.com/pod-product-compliance
Lightning Source LLC
Chambersburg PA
CBHW071416040426

42444CB00009B/2275